QUARTER-MILE
Chaos
Images of Drag Racing Mayhem

Steve Reyes

CarTech®

CarTech®

CarTech®, Inc.
838 Lake Street South
Forest Lake, MN 55025
Phone: 651-277-1200 or 800-551-4754
Fax: 651-277-1203
www.cartechbooks.com

Edit by Josh Brown
Layout by Katie Sonmor

ISBN 978-1-61325-594-0
Item No. CT677

Library of Congress Cataloging-in-Publication Data

Reyes, Steve.
  Quarter-mile chaos / by Steve Reyes.
    p. cm.
  Includes index.
  ISBN 1-932494-25-1 (HARDCOVER)
  1. Automobiles, Racing--Pictorial works. I. Title.

TL236.R475 2005
629.228'022'2--dc22   2005017252

Written, edited, and designed in the U.S.A.
Printed in China
10 9 8 7 6 5 4 3 2 1

Front Cover:

Orange County International Raceway, October 1970

Mike Kuhl and Billy Tidwell had just returned from the NHRA Indy Nationals. At that event, Tidwell made a run and his parachute opened late. He proceeded to run off the end of the track and into the ABC Wide World of Sports remote camera set there. The camera tumbled down onto the nose of the Top Fuel dragster, ruining the paint and body. On returning to California, I asked Mike and Bill if they would like to do a fire burnout and try to get a cover on a major magazine. The two talked it over and decided, "Hey, we already screwed up the racecar body and paint, let's burn up the rest."

So we met at OCIR with four gallons of gas and matches. We did two okay burnouts, which were nothing outstanding. What you see on the cover is the third and final attempt. Billy pulled the Top Fueler into the OCIR bleach box. Coming to a stop in the bleach box, a crewman named "Fats" started pouring the big bucket of gas. I was waving to Mike to move the push truck out of the background. Fats doused the headers with gas and WOOF! The world became orange, yellow, and red. Tidwell sat with his head down watching the cockpit fill with fire. Then he decided to go. He came by me with the car's body and chute pack on fire.

All told, I got my photo, all the paint and the chute pack burned off, Fats had no hair on his arms, Tidwell's firesuit was a little darker, and OCIR had a mini-crater melted into its bleach box. *Hot Rod* magazine thought the photo was too strong, but *Popular Hot Rodding* thought different – the picture was the cover in January 1971.

Title Page:

OCIR, California, 1972

Top Fuel vet Larry Bowers suffers the ultimate clutch and engine failure. Larry was okay, but parts struck and injured a fan who was walking in the pits. This photo came about because I was called across the racetrack and couldn't get back to the photo area.

Back Cover, Main:

Indy, mid-1980s

Okay, another 1980s funny car happening. Ron Dudley in the Oklahoma-based *St. Moritz* fuel funny car. Then, BOOM! The fuel tank explodes and all hell breaks loose. The body blows off, that was good for Ron, as it took lots of fire off the driver. Ron was singed, but he walked away.

Back Cover, Inset:

Union Grove, Wisconsin, early 1990s

Great Lakes manager Bob Metzler always knew how to entertain his crowds. Attending one of his drag-race, monster-truck, jet-car, stunt extravaganzas, I clicked this human-torch photo. I was told this "stuntman" arrived with a Vega in tow. He made a deal with Metzler and the next thing I know he was sitting in a gas-soaked suit in a broken-down junk Vega. The door was closed and his assistant lit the fire. The Vega was an instant inferno and about 10 seconds later he came out ablaze from the burning Vega. He threw himself on the ground and his assistant put him out. He got to his feet and the crowd cheered!

OVERSEAS DISTRIBUTION BY:

Europe
PGUK
63 Hatton Garden
London EC1N 8LE, England
Phone: 020 7061 1980 • Fax: 020 7242 3725
www.pguk.co.uk

Canada
Login Canada
300 Saulteaux Crescent
Winnipeg, MB, R3J 3T2 Canada
Phone: 800 665 1148 • Fax: 800 665 0103
www.lb.ca

Australia
Renniks Publications Ltd.
3/37-39 Green Street
Banksmeadow, NSW 2109, Australia
Phone: 2 9695 7055 • Fax: 2 9695 7355
www.renniks.com

CONTENTS

Dedication

For my wife, Bethany, and my daughters, Ashley, Haley, and Emily.
Love ya, and thanks.

ACKNOWLEDGMENTS

My thanks to every man and woman who ever strapped themselves into a racecar. Without you, this book would not exist. Also, to Don Gillespie, whose darkroom work helped make this possible.

PREFACE

The Golden Years – that's what I believe my photos represent. The years drag racing started to grow and mature. When I started to shoot my photos, it was still a sport where fathers, sons, brothers, and neighbors joined together and went racing. Backyard race-cars could still make their mark in this sport. Drivers were fearless and drove by the seat of their pants. Racetracks flourished throughout the United States. "Match race madness" was the disease of the day.

Since I was born in Northern California, a few more NorCal racers are featured within these pages. Those guys kept me alive by buying my photos, dragging me along in the back of pickup trucks to shoot my race photos, slipping me an extra $20 when I needed film – yep, them NorCal guys looked out for me.

Enjoy the photos. I enjoyed shooting them.

ABOUT THE AUTHOR

It was 1963 in Northern California. The ad in the *Oakland Tribune* screamed, "Come See Nitro Burning Slingshot Dragsters at Fremont Drag Strip!" That was my first contact with the strange and exciting sport of organized drag racing. The ad made the sport sound like the greatest thing since sliced bread. Being 15 years old at the time, I had to see it to believe it.

I begged and bugged my dad until he finally gave in to the nagging. We piled into the Rambler wagon and headed the 30 miles to Fremont Drag Strip. Armed with my dad's 620 Brownie, I was ready to record these freaks of the asphalt.

Mesmerizing is the only way to describe my first day at the racetrack. The smoke, noise, and nitro fumes were addicting to this wide-eyed teenager. I was hooked, and soon added an old Eumig 8-mm camera to my photo gear. Now I was ready to shoot some photos! But a couple of weekends shooting behind the fence with all the other spectators didn't cut it. So after a talk with Ron Lawrence, the track manager, and a little stretching of the truth, I was in the photo area!

Shooting photos in the Fremont photo area was a very interesting experience, and an insurance broker's nightmare. No guardrails or walls – just me, my camera, and a bunch of crazies in their nitro-burning missiles on the wide-open spaces of Fremont Drag Strip. I don't think it was courage that drove me to shoot photos out there – just being 15 and bulletproof was enough. The movies I shot were cool, but I really loved to stop the motion with a still camera. My still-camera stash was sad, a 620 Brownie and an Instamatic 126 with a wind-up motor drive.

However, I did manage to pan and get some very cool motor-drive pictures. Frank Bradley was driving the Bailey Brothers *Dragmaster* A/FD at the time. Being a show-off, I showed him my pictures. To my amazement, he wanted to buy the photos! All of a sudden I had money in my pocket. So if racers like photos, I thought, I must be able to profit from this.

I was soon able to purchase a 35-mm camera and a few lenses. I didn't get rid of my 8-mm movie camera, heck no. I built a mount for it and it took various rides on the Top Fuel dragsters of Don Cook, Rich Zoucha, the Whiz Kids, and Roger Harrington. Either on the roll bar or on the front end, my movie camera recorded some cool stuff in the mid-1960s.

Purchasing *Drag News* at the Fremont concession stand on a weekly basis brought me closer to the wild world of West Coast and national drag races. Reading every story and studying every photo gave me the notion that there were a whole lot of cars out there to see and photograph.

Sending photos to *Drag News* helped me gain respect from the Northern California racers. Suddenly photos of them were appearing weekly in *Drag News*, *National Dragster*, *Drag Digest*, and *Drag World*. My photo beat included Fremont, Half Moon Bay, Lodi, Sacramento, Salinas, and Fresno. These tracks were my stomping grounds. Many big-name racers ran at Fremont when they toured the West Coast. I was able to see them and hopefully get a photo. I was allowed to shoot the weekly events at Fremont, but not the big events.

Not able to shoot at my home track, I went where the racecars were – Bakersfield! In 1965 or 1966, *Drag News* arranged for me to have a photo pass at the Smokers Event. I begged, borrowed, and borrowed some more to attend the event. However, I had no credentials on arrival at the track. I was 200 miles from home and all the money I had in the world was in my pocket. So I paid my way in. Sitting in the stands on the starting line sucked – too many people were in my way. Having never shot there before, I decided to pack up and head for the finish line. Well, at least nobody was in my way. It was cool! Engine explosions! Blower explosions! These were cool action pictures and I was sitting in the stands. I processed my film as soon as I got home, made some prints, and sent them off to Mike Dougherty at *Drag Racing Magazine*. Soon after I found these pictures published in the 1966 *Drag Racing Almanac*. From then on, thanks to Mike, I had credentials wherever I wanted to go.

Doris Herbert of *Drag News* and I patched things up over the Bakersfield screw-up, and I ended up working for her on a regular basis, covering major NHRA, AHRA, and IHRA races. Doris gave me great advice on how to cover national events. Thank you, Ms. Herbert!

Making your living as a drag-racing photographer wasn't easy in the 1960s, but thanks to the support of NorCal racers and magazines I was able to travel the ever-widening drag-race circuit. In 1967 I became the NHRA's Division 7 photographer/reporter, which was a nice perk. I covered what was then the hotbed of the drag-racing world, Southern California. The constant driving over three years between Northern and Southern California was unacceptable. The writing was on the wall, so I moved to Southern California. The move allowed me to be close to the Southern California racetracks and magazines, and to the folks who built the cars I photographed. Yes, it was a struggle at first, but with my Hasselblad and a new Nikon motor drive, I was ready to conquer the world.

Soon after moving to Los Angeles, the phone rang. It was Revell, the model/toy people. For some strange reason they called me to photograph their venture into drag racing, which was Whipple & McCullouch's funny car. I met up with Art and Ed and we shot some photos. I guess Revell liked me, because I ended up shooting quite a few other Revell-sponsored cars.

I then struck up a friendship with Kenny Youngblood and Don Kirby. Kenny is one of the best (if not the best) artists ever when it comes to racecars. Don was building state-of-the-art funny-car bodies. Enter yours truly: "Would you like some ink on your racecar?" I was there to provide my services and to promote Kirby & Youngblood. Those were great times. I met many a racer and shot many a photo. I remember that in one month in 1973, out of 11 drag-racing magazines on the newsstand, eight of the covers were mine. Not bad for a freelance guy from Northern California.

All that crazy freelance stuff stopped on October 31, 1973. I was offered a real job with Argus Publishing. Argus had decided to offer me a job because it was cheaper to hire me than to retain me as a freelance photographer. They made me an offer I couldn't refuse – salary, plus benefits and expenses for travel to races. Yahoo! The freelance market was weakening due to magazine failures and racetrack closings. I spent 20 years and four months at Argus, travelling to every state in the union and every province in Canada. I toured England with Raymond Beadle and the *Blue Max* AA/FC team, and made two trips to Japan, Australia, and New Zealand with the crazy monster-truck guys. I photographed the World of Outlaws and Ascot CRA Sprints when I could. Bonneville? You bet!

Reggie Jackson of the New York Yankees had some cars for me to photograph. After shooting his cars he asked me to shoot baseball, so from 1981 to 1985 I did Major League Baseball. Reggie introduced me to the curator of the Baseball Hall of Fame in Cooperstown, New York. I ended up doing photos for them and received a lifetime pass to Cooperstown to prove it. Eat your heart out, Pete Rose!

After many a drag race, car show, etc., I became interested in something other than cars. My wife dragged me to an NHL Los Angeles Kings game. I found it very interesting and very fast. Yes, I needed to shoot photos of this sport. Well, after much tap dancing, phone calls, and begging, I managed a photo pass. I guess I was in the right place at the right time. I ended up photographing hockey between 1991 and 1995 for Bruce Bennett Studios. Trading cards, posters, New York-based magazine covers, photo shoots of NHL stars' homes, I got to do it all. And yes, I was still doing my regular gig at Argus.

My job at Argus ended in 1994. Argus was downsizing and I was it. They gave me my tour van, which had a million miles on it, I bought my camera gear for 10 cents on the dollar, got a cash settlement, and see ya! I was a freelancer again. The editors at Argus weren't happy to see the one guy who produced more photo features than anyone being shown the door. They looked out for me and I continued to receive some great assignments.

Freelancing is a great crap shoot. Over the past 10 years, I have shot drag racing, naked girls on Harleys, tattoo conventions, and all kinds of strange and wonderful things. My photos have been used not only by Mattel for their model kits but for a great number of the Johnny Lightning/Playing Mantis die-cast drag racing and muscle cars.

Drag-racing photography has always been my true love. I have acquired thousands of photos that span decades and it seems a shame to leave them all boxed up. So I have put together this book of my favorite action shots to show the excitement and danger of the sport to drag-racing fans everywhere. To me the glory days of this sport are gone, but the photos of a bygone era are here to stay.

INTRODUCTION

Some consider drag racing to be a violent yet beautiful sport. This book, *Quarter-Mile Chaos*, portrays what I call the good ol' days of drag racing. This was a time when racing was about creating a racecar that would get from point A to point B without blowing up. There were no large corporate sponsors or a lot of safety rules and equipment; just a bunch of owners, builders, and drivers who wanted to build the fastest car around, and a certain photographer who wanted to capture the photo that depicted the sport in a way that no one else could. Oftentimes that photo portrayed a beautiful chaos that drag fans and non-drag fans alike could relate to.

Back in the good ol' days there were no guardrails or walls, and "if you get hit, too bad" was the normal attitude. Armed with a couple of cameras and some film, I wandered the quarter-mile. While most spectators thought the drivers were nuts to pilot these nitro-guzzling missiles, the drivers I knew told me I was nuts to stand out there hoping for that one special photo. I guess we agreed we were all crazy, but we had fun.

Staying alive among these four-wheeled, mini-atomic bombs was always a challenge. Being young and fearless at the time probably helped, or it could have been that I was just blind to the danger factor. All I know is that I wanted that certain photo – the action photo no one else had captured.

Getting that cool explosion photo was nice, but ducking the parts was another story. I sometimes felt like I had a target on my back. When parts and pieces go zinging by at 200 mph, you do wish to be elsewhere. The one thing I learned over the years is to not run. Duck, yes. Run, no. Over all those years of shooting, I've had hot oil sprayed all over me and have been hit in the foot by a piece of a clutch plate. That was it. Did I have a guardian angel? You bet I did. My Hawaiian shirt and Levis had no bulletproofing or special powers. Without my guardian angel I would have looked like a piece of Swiss cheese the first year I was shooting.

To capture any sport on film you must study it. Drag racing is no exception. Knowing a driver's style of driving and the way a nitro engine worked was key to this photographer's success. Not knowing your subjects is a waste of time and film. I would be at the finish line 1,320 feet away and when two cars staged on the starting line, I could tell you which one would explode and which would finish the quarter-mile run. Am I a mind reader? No, it's just knowing and studying my subjects, with a little luck thrown in for good measure.

The photos in this book show the chaotic side of drag racing. Yes, the cars do explode and they do crash. However, thanks to all the safety gear drivers wear, and strong, well-built cars, most of the time it was only their wallets that received injuries.

Fire is beautiful to photograph but deadly to drivers. Yet there is a sense of humor to fire that is strange. For instance, Leroy Goldstein (driver of the Ramchargers funny car) got tired of being surprised by fire, so he had small windows installed in the firewall of his car. He wasn't concerned about fire per se, he just wanted to see a preview of the fire that was about to occur.

Most drivers will tell you their job is to get from point A to point B as fast as they can without blowing up. In the early days, this caused drivers and photographers many a thrill. They smoked the tires, drove off the racetrack, exploded, and caught fire, and yet still had to get to the finish line. I must admit these guys were my heroes. Not only did I get some wild photos, but I was able to make them famous as well.

The wildest class to photograph was the 98-inch wheelbase fuel altered roadsters. Stuff a blown, fuel-burning Hemi into a 98-inch wheelbase roadster and hang on. These were the cars that brought Top Fuel drivers and funny-car drivers to the fence to watch. Wheelstands, sideways, half-mile runs on quarter-mile tracks – you name it, these cars did it. Northern California gave birth to one of the wildest in the class – Rich Guasco's *Pure Hell* Bantam roadster, which was driven by a mild-mannered Okie, Dale "The Snail" Emory. Southern California had its own brand of wild fuel-altered driver, Wild Willie Borsch. The guys who drove in this class have a special place in my memories. They tried many a time to run me over and throw parts at me, but to me they are a part of a bygone era of drag racing.

No matter how much safety is put into drag racing, you always have the human factor. Drivers want to go fast and win. Engine tuners want to go fast and win. Big corporate sponsors add more pressure to win and win big. So cars are run on the edge, tuned to the last 1,320 feet – no more, no less. The stakes are high in the world of drag racing.

In the days of old, you blew up, put another home-built motor in, and you made the next round. With the high cost of parts and engines today, only the high-dollar teams can compete. Yes, the days of 120 Top Fuel dragsters (Bakersfield Smokers) or the 64 funny-car manufacturer meets (Orange County International Raceway) are only a fond memory for us "nitroholics."

All my "chaos" photos in this book have something in common. They may look wild and crazy, but no one was seriously injured. Sure, a few bumps and bruises, but everyone walked away. All in all I had a great time getting to know the drivers and engine builders of that bygone time. Although the golden era of drag racing is gone, I was lucky to be there to capture it on film. Many a driver and owner learned from my photos. A few drivers and car builders would joke, "Please don't go to the finish line when I run." But my motto was, "We have the photos," and I made sure we did.

Fremont, California, 1971
The engine leaned out a bit at the finish line, and BOOM! Instant Jr. Fueler. The beautiful *California Charger* of John Keeling and Jerry Clayton needed a new top on the engine. Driver Rick Ramsey ducked, so he was okay.

Fremont, California, 1967
Phil Nunez had a few problems with the Nunez and Dillon AA/GS Willys. It kind of got away from him at the finish line. Phil walked away, but the Willys was dragged away by the track tow-truck, never to race again.

Indy, 1973
Harlan Thompson has his own private cookout in Jerry Baltes' *Tom and Jerry* fuel funny Mustang. Harlan wasn't hurt, but the car needed some TLC.

Pomona, California, 1971
Punxsutawney Phil? No, it's the driver of the Lopez and Mumford Super Stock Nova. He's wondering if help is on the way. The Nova went back to its home in Dallas, Texas, slightly bent. Thankfully nobody was hurt.

Irwindale, California, 1974
NorCal veteran Top Fuel racer Larry "Shorty" Leventon ventured into the SoCal Top Fuel wars. "Shorty" had some major blower problems on his fuel-burning Chevy engine.

Indy, 1973
Shirley Muldowney was convinced to switch over to Top Fuel after this fuel funny-car inferno. Shirley got a little crispy in this one. When she returned, her rear-engine Top Fueler was just fine, thank you. In top fuel, the fire is behind you.

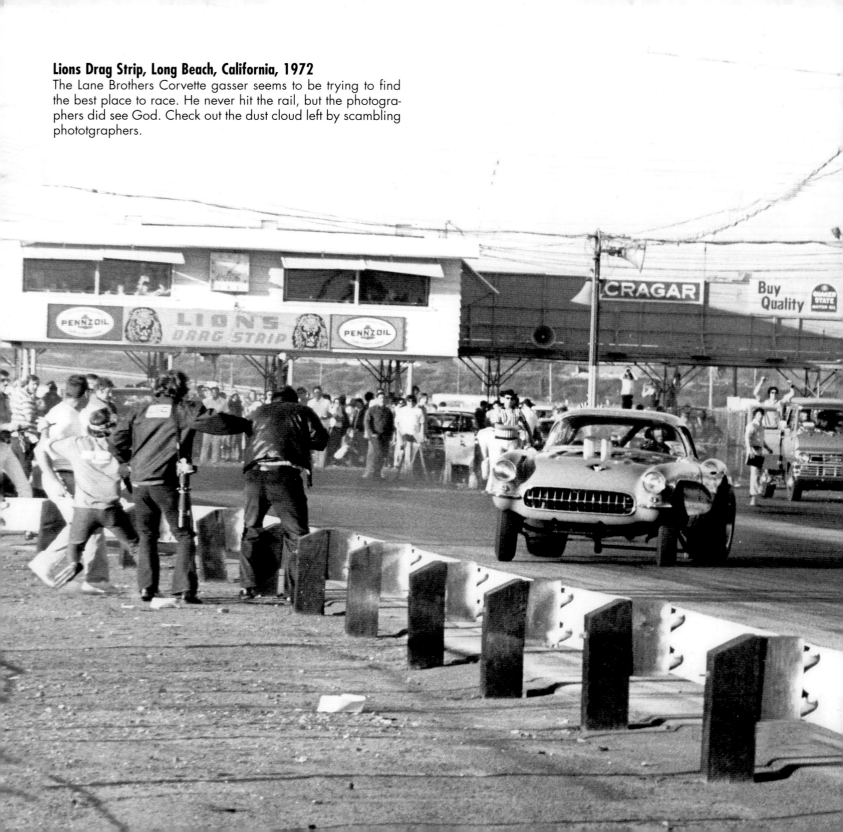

Lions Drag Strip, Long Beach, California, 1972
The Lane Brothers Corvette gasser seems to be trying to find the best place to race. He never hit the rail, but the photographers did see God. Check out the dust cloud left by scambling phototgraphers.

Gainesville, Florida, 1972
Jim "Superman" Nicoll lights up the Speed Equipment World Fuel Vega. Nicoll bailed out in the shut-off area when the roof started to melt on him. He bounced a bit, but was not injured. The car, however, was really well done.

OCIR, California, 1972

Tom Prock joins the funny-car conga line with the *Custom Body* Mopar-bodied AA/FC. In the first photo, the photographer is my old Northern California buddy Mike Bagnod. He's clicking a color page for *Drag Racing USA* magazine. In the second photo, the photographer with the camera on his shoulder is Hall of Fame member Jim Kelly. Hey, when your lens is too long, you gotta watch.

Lions Drag Strip, Long Beach, California, 1972
That's Jack Martin in the Penner, Beech, and Martin Top Fueler about to go over backwards. Yes, he crashed and destroyed the new dragster. He walked away from the mangled racecar.

Fremont, California, 1968-69
NorCal racer Nick Otto purchased *The Warlock* from Fred Sorensen. Nick had Frank Pitts at the controls. Frank was very exciting behind the wheel. Sadly for everyone, Pitts crashed *The Warlock* at Sacto, California, and received serious injuries. *The Warlock* was destroyed, never to thrill again.

Englishtown, New Jersey, 1971
If your funny car won't run on asphalt, try the grass. Omar "The Tentmaker" Carruthers turns his full funny car into the world's fastest lawn mower. Omar didn't hurt anything, but I made money on the photos.

Las Vegas, Nevada, 1971
When the roof collapses on your funny car, just aim for the photographers in the shutdown area. Mike Miller did, but he missed us. The roof popped back up.

OCIR, California, 1968
Looks like the *Parts Mart* fuel funny Camaro needs a part right now. Driver/owner Kip Brundage seems to be puzzled by the wheel's disappearance.

West Salem, Ohio Dragway 42, 1972

"The Bounty Huntress" Shirley Muldowney versus Fritz Callier in the CKC Vega. Shirley's Mustang lit up at the 1,000-foot mark. The fuel funny looked like a meteor at the finish line. The car veered off the track and rolled, ending right-side up. Shirley received burns on her hands and around her eyes, but was at the track the next day. These photos were shot one-handed, as I had a drink in my left hand. This was one of the worst funny-car fires at the time.

Gainesville, Florida, 1973
Don "The Snake" Prudhomme boils the tires on his *Feather* Top Fuel dragster. This car was one of the winningest cars Prudhomme owned and drove.

Lions Drag Strip, Long Beach, California, 1967

Lew Arrington had serious transmission problems off the Lions starting line. His *Brutus* GTO fuel funny car exploded at the green glow of the Christmas tree. Lew climbed out uninjured, and there were no injuries to fans from red-hot flying metal. Lew was racing Dickie Harrell. All the other photographers ran to Harrell's side, but I stayed on Lew's side. He's a NorCal guy and always supported me by buying my pictures. So I was the only one who got the photo.

Lakeland, Florida, 1972
Ron Potter slammed hard into the Lakeland Raceway guardrail while driving his *Golden Nugget* fuel funny Mustang. Ron suffered serious head injuries. He never returned to driving again.

Fremont, California, 1972
Pete's Lil' Demon versus Smokey Joe Lee. Things got hot for *Demon* driver Leroy "Doc" Hales. Hales got the hot *Demon* stopped, and exited quickly. If Hales got burned, he could administer his own first aid – he was a paramedic.

Martin, Michigan, 1972
Fire burnouts are cool, but not if they're done by accident. Here, Ronnie Martin lights up the bleach box and surprises a bunch of people. The very flammable VHT was often used for burnouts. A little on the headers and, WOOF! No one was hurt. Ironically, Martin crashed and totaled Robert Anderson's Top Fueler the next day. See page 112.

Lions Drag Strip, Long Beach, California, 1971
Fred Badburg ran one of the baddest A/SRs. This was the debut of his new Cerny paint job. I photographed the car prior to the race. My ladder fell on the back of the racecar, putting a big scratch in the new paint. I told Fred I would pay to fix it, he said okay. On this run, he smacked the guardrail and destroyed the fenders and paint. He told me not to worry about the scratch.

OCIR, California, 1972
The driver of this rolling barbecue was Ron Fassel. *The Elephant Hunter* Mustang was one nasty inferno. The Phoenix-based team took home one very charred fuel funny car and one driver with some very serious burns on his hands. Do you see the primer on the car body? That's from a fire the week before.

Irwindale, California, 1972
"Fearless" Fred Goeske puts four wheels in the air with his fuel funny Vega. Yes, the car got hurt when it came down.

Fremont, California, 1971

Joe Winters sets the launch record for a funny car body. His *Swinger* fuel funny's body seemed to hang forever in the Northern California skies. Joe was the only one-legged funny-car driver I ever came across, although I believe Chuck Finders drove after losing a leg in a drag-racing accident.

Tulsa, Oklahoma, 1972
Jake Johnston driving Gene Snow's *Revell Snowman 2* blue
Charger fuel funny car lights up at the finish line. Jake was
okay, but the blue Charger was singed.

OCIR, California, 1972

Top Fuel vet Larry Bowers suffers the ultimate clutch and engine failure. Larry was okay, but parts struck and injured a fan who was walking in the pits. This photo came about because I was called across the racetrack and couldn't get back to the photo area.

Indy, 1978
Billy Graham and his *Million Dollar Baby* fuel funny car have a body latch problem. Graham finished the weekend with lots of silver tape.

Ontario, California, 1972
Shirl Geer is in big trouble in his *Chain Lightning* fuel funny Mustang. Shirl suffered serious burns, but returned the next day. With hands bandaged and car body patched up, he was able to run the first round of elimination and win the world championship for fuel funny cars NHRA-style.

Inset: OCIR, California, 1972
One run, that's all Jim Peace got in the Bratton, Peace, & Handa Top Fuel dragster. The then-new fueler suffered a transmission and clutch explosion. The explosion cut the back of the car off, sending Peace into a rear-wheelless slide into the shutoff area. Peace walked away, but the car was junk.

Lakeland, Florida, 1972
Don Garlits lights up the Florida night. T. C. Lemmons and his bottle of highly flammable VHT, a liquid compound used for cars to spin tires in, can be blamed for many a crispy bleach box.

Tulsa, Oklahoma, 1972

John "Cogo" Eads gives a new meaning to "fireball" with his fuel funny car. Unable to see because of the fire, he plowed into the rear of the *Vulture* fuel funny car. The bodies of both cars came off. This actually helped Cogo – with the body off the fire wasn't as bad. Cogo had a few burns, and *Vulture* driver Henry Harrison was very unhappy.

Lakeland, Florida, 1972
Richard Holcomb hit the throttle on his Top Fuel dragster and
BOOM! No more bottom end. Lots of pieces and fire, but
thankfully nobody was hurt.

Englishtown, New Jersey, 1972
The Cyr & Schofield Top Fueler tries to become a sidewinder at the finish line. The engine tried to jump out of the chassis. Driver Flip Schofield got the car stopped okay and the San Diego, California-based team had a long tow home.

Las Vegas, Nevada, 1971
NorCal racecar builder and driver Dave Uyehara has big handling problems with his brand new Top Fuel dragster. All the parts and pieces missed me, and Dave walked away. However, the car was totaled.

Pomona, California, 1968 or 1969
Is Connie Kalitta's newest invention a Top Fuel car that can drive around corners? No, sadly Connie had problems firing the car on the fire-up road. He found a steel pole at the turn before the quarter-mile. The car bent, the pole didn't. Connie wasn't injured, but his wallet was wounded.

Indy, 1971
Ronnie Martin goes for a wild ride in Robert Anderson's Top Fuel dragster. He almost came down on yours truly. I think the ground moved when he hit the racetrack.

Inset: Ontario, California, 1970

Does your Top Fueler have handling problems? Maybe keeping all the wheels on the ground would help. An unknown Top Fueler becomes a tricycle just past the finish line. It stopped okay; no harm, no foul.

Fremont, California, 1966

This is one of my own personal favorite drag action photos – Bill Dunlap driving Jon Halsted's Top Gas dragster. The coolest thing about this photo, besides the wheelstand, is the airbrush effect in the background. A car in the near lane smoked Dunlap in. The smoke passed Dunlap and hung on the grandstands when he did his thing. This was the first of two giant wheelstands on this run.

Below: Ontario, California, 1972

Funny car versus concrete guardrail: concrete wall - 1, funny car - 0. I believe the driver was Preston Davis. He was okay, but embarrassed.

Ontario, California, 1971
Roger "Ramjet" Gates gets torched while driving his *Cracklin' Rose* Top Fuel dragster. Roger escaped serious burns thanks to a great firesuit. He got the car stopped, even though the chutes burned off. I believe Roger returned to his Bonneville car after this cookout.

Atco, New Jersey, early 1980s
On tour with New York City ace photographer Norman Blake, we came upon Doug Rose and his *Green Mamba* jet car. Doug had a problem — no pit crew. His local pit crew was a no-show. So, heck, if I drive a tow car, I can start a jet car. That evening I became the pit crew/photographer. After the match race we ran, the fun began. The track dragged out an old Japanese-made passenger car, we chained it to the back of the *Mamba*, I got my camera, and Doug hit the afterburner. The result was lots of fire and flying hot metal.

Lions Drag Strip, Long Beach, California, 1972
The *Avengers* Top Fueler of Brissette and Noice explodes off the Lions starting line. Veteran Top Fuel driver Bob Noice handled the Jim Brissette horsepower.

Martin, Michigan, early 1970s
"The Mandrill" Steve Carbone on tour with his own Top Fueler. Carbone seemed to drive everything in the SoCal area. Top Gas, Top Fuel, whatever. Okay, how many of you readers knew Carbone even drove for Pete Robinson?

Scottsdale, Arizona, 1970
Subbing for Chris Karamesines, Cliff Zink heads for the stars with The Greek's Top Fuel dragster. Zink ground a hole in the driver's seat and destroyed the front end and wheels on landing.

Pomona, California, 1972

Greg Bellemeur chops down the Christmas tree with the Bellemeur and Rob Phillips *Easy Rider* Fiat. Greg did a great job on the tree. Unfortunately, the tree fought back and conked the driver on the head, giving Greg a massive headache and leaving a track worker to pick up the pieces.

Pomona, California, 1972
If the *Easy Rider* can do it, so can Don Waite. In an almost back-to-back chopping of the Christmas tree, Don Waite driving his A/A roadster blasts the newly installed tree. Those altereds were always hard on the Christmas trees. The cars sure kept that track worker busy that day!

Indy, 1972

The finish-line tower is like a vulture's perch for photographers. Standing up there can be fun. Just before flyin' Phil Castronovo blew the Custom Auto Body fuel funny car to pieces, a photographer for *Life* magazine asked me which car to shoot. I told him the car in the far lane. Well, I got my photos and Castronovo appeared as a two-page spread in *Life* magazine. I just love being right.

OCIR, California, 1971
Though I got smoked in by the car on the other side, coming out of the smoke cloud is a very crossed-up "Flash" Gordon Mineo. Flash tattooed the guardrail head on. He wasn't hurt, but his fuel funny Vega was shorter.

Martin, Michigan, 1972
"Big Daddy" Don Garlits is at it again. His fire burnouts were always the best.
His crew chief T. C. Lemmons was a master of the inferno with his bottle of VHT
– look out!

Gainesville, Florida, 1972
Clayton Harris has a major meltdown with Jack McKay's *New Dimension* Top Fuel dragster. Parts and pieces of the blower and engine rained through the Florida air. This boom must have woken up every sleeping gator in Florida.

Tulsa, Oklahoma, 1972

Larry Brown experienced the ultimate engine failure with the Bob Dumont Top Fuel dragster. The Top Fueler spit its whole engine out of the frame rails at the finish-line lights. Parts and pieces were everywhere. Part of the rear tire flew over my head, but that just gave me a little shade that day. No people got hurt, but Bob Dumont's wallet sure did.

Pomona, California, 1972

The late Jim Bucher took the "breaking" in of his new Top Fuel Chevy dragster one step too far. Not a great way to debut a new racecar. Jim took his bent racer back home to Ohio and fixed it.

Gainesville, Forida 1972
The eastern James Warren and his blown Chevy-powered Top Fueler had valve-cover problems. He lost a valve cover and it put oil on the hot headers, then, WOOF!

Bakersfield, California, 1967
Frank Pitts purchased the *Lizard* Top Fueler of Bishop, Herbert, and Raynor. He had problems on the push-down road. The car made a quick move when it fired, and turned into a spectator fence. The car was bent a bit, but Frank was okay.

Irwindale, California, 1971 or 1972
Tom Tolar, at the wheel of the Tolar and Tolbert Top Fuel dragster, has engine problems. The *TNT Special* spit its engine out about 400 feet into its run, making it very exciting for this photographer. I got the oil bath and Tom had his hands full stopping the motorless racecar. Tom wasn't hurt, and I will never rust.

OCIR, California, 1972

"The Northwest Terror," Herm Petersen, finds trouble in his Petersen and Fitz Top Fuel dragster. Herm lost a rear wheel about 300 feet out. The car flipped and slid backwards almost the entire quarter-mile. The fuel tank, which was mounted behind the driver, popped open. The burning fuel bathed Herm. He received very serious facial burns as well as burns on his hands.

Irwindale, California, 1970

Fire burnouts are cool, but only if you know you are going to do one. Norm Ries' fire burnout wasn't planned. The crewman pouring VHT splashed it onto the headers and WOOF! Note that the bleach bottle is on fire as well as his pants. It makes for cool pictures, but it's dangerous. Nobody got hurt at the surprise barbecue.

Pomona, California, 1970
Norm Wilcox mows down the finish-line timing lights with the Wilcox and Levy Top Gas dragster. I think he's racing a concerned Bill Mullins, driving his Alabama-based twin.

Martin, Michigan, 1972
The man in the flying Top Fuel dragster is Ronnie Martin. The car belonged to Robert Anderson. I photographed it when it was new and fresh. Now I had photos of its demise. Ronnie limped away, but the car was a total wreck. He was racing Carl Olson.

112

Indy, 1972
Danny Johnson has high-speed wobble in the front forks of his fuel-burning Harley drag bike. There goes the front wheel at 160 mph. Now it's slide for life for Danny. The bike destroys itself by hitting and going over the guardrail. Danny gets up and strolls away. Those Harley guys are tough!

114

Fremont, California, 1972
Jim Peace had some major fuel-tank problems with his AA/FA. The Fremont, California-based car may look familiar. It's the original *Pure Hell* AA/FA Chrysler-powered car.

Bristol, Tennessee, 1968
It's a hot time on the starting line for Bob Gibson. Gibson is at the controls of Raymond Godman's *Tennessee BoWeevil* Top Fuel dragster. Godman's Top Fueler was well known in the Southeast. Memphis, Tennessee, was the *BoWeevil's* home.

Ontario, California, mid-1970s
Bill Spevacek lights up his Mopar-bodied fuel funny car at the 1,000-foot mark. The fire got going good. Then, whoosh!, the body flew off and went over the spectator fence. The fire went out and Bill stopped his Northwest-based racer. Nobody was smashed by the flying body.

Great Lakes Dragway, Union Grove, Wisconsin, late 1970s
It's that showman of the Midwest, "Broadway Bob." Here Bob takes a little ride on the nose of Doug Rose's *Green Mamba* jet dragster. Bob was the manager/promoter at the Grove. Yeah, he could promote some classic drag races, kinda like pro wrestling.

OCIR, California, late 1970s to early 1980s
Gary Cornwall cleans the top of the engine of the Cornwall Brothers *Battleborn* Top Fuel dragster. Nobody was hurt, just the Nevada team's wallet.

Lions Drag Strip, Long Beach, California, 1971
Dennis Geisler exploded from the starting line in the Geisler and Graf AA/FA. "Glassman" Geisler also drove the *Hindsight* funny car and a funny car of his own.

Fremont, California, 1966

A major explosion right off the starting line left the Juggors racing team without a bell housing and clutch. The driver escaped injury. I was hit in the side by a piece of clutch. The piece went in my jacket pocket and spun me around. I was sore, but hey, send in another Top Fueler.

OCIR, California, 1968
Bobby Hightower has a few tire issues with Dale Smart's Top Fuel dragster. The veteran driver got the car stopped with no problems.

Ontario, California, mid-1970s
Independent funny-car owner/driver Jeff Courtie has a major "boom" with his fuel 'Cuda. Jeff wasn't hurt, but the 'Cuda needed a new fiberglass body and supercharger. Jeff's ears are still ringing.

Thompson, Ohio
I can't remember the year I first came across Bob Motz and his awesome J-79-powered jet truck. But once you saw his truck in action, you didn't forget it. Shaking ground, lots of fire – those are the Motz trademarks. It was a very cool show.

Irwindale, California, 1971

Dave Hough and his *Nanook* AA/FA are at it again. Dave proves that what goes up must come down. If you look close at the car's return to earth photo, the steering rod has broken. Having no steering is no problem for an AA/FA driver. Dave finished the pass – 180 mph with no steering!

Martin, Michigan, early 1970s
Shirley Muldowney lights up the Michigan night with her famed pink Top Fueler. This fire burnout was an accident. The bleach box was ignited by the pink fueler's hot head... er, pipes.

OCIR, California, 1971

The world's fastest mailman, Arly Langlo, finds lots of bite with the *Zip Code* Top Fuel dragster, a bucks-down Top Fuel racer. Arly seemed to be on fire or wheels in the air every run.

Irwindale, California, 1971-72

My ol' buddy Dave Hough and *The Mighty Nanook* AA/FA. Dave was always up for anything. So I went and got permission from the Hermosa Beach City Hall to do an AA/FA parachute photo on the main street of Hermosa Beach, California. On that fateful day, we had the mayor and city council folks lining the main street and, of course, police for crowd control. The street was cleared and the sidewalks were packed with people. Here comes Dave and *Nanook* as the engine comes to life. Dave stops to warm the engine. I get in place, camera in hand. Okay, now Dave is to drive down the street, 45 to 60 mph and pull his chutes. An AA/FA with twin chutes blossomed on a city street, cool pic, right? I smell another cover for me and the *Nanook*.

I'm in place, Dave's in place. Dave hits the throttle like it's the final round at the nationals. *Nanook's* tires explode into smoke, Dave pulls the chute levers, and they blossom. Unfortunately, someone has forgotten to put in the main pin mounting the chutes to the car. Yes, they blossom and fall to the ground. Meanwhile, Dave is not feeling the chutes and has the pedal to the metal. He blazes by me boiling the tires sideways. Okay, now here's the picture, AA/FA boiling the tires on the city street with the mayor, etc., looking on. It gets better – this street runs east-west, and *Nanook* is going west toward the Pacific Ocean. Dave goes through two intersections, where *Nanook* has the green light. Dave blows through the red on the third. I think that the people heard him coming and stopped. Just past the third intersection the road drops and becomes a hill, then a curve, then if you don't turn – Pacific Ocean.

I saw Dave and the *Nanook* disappear over the top of the hill and knew that Dave was going swimming with the fishes. We all jumped into *Nanook's* push car and followed the smoke trail and tracks. Over the hill we went down towards the ocean, no *Nanook*. About half a mile down the Pacific Coast Highway, parked on the side of the highway, was the *Nanook*.

Dave wasn't excited, he couldn't figure out why we were excited. No, we didn't try another chute photo. I put a police car behind the AA/FA, had him write Dave a ticket, and a *Popular Hot Rodding* cover was born.

Union Grove, Wisconsin, early 1990s
Great Lakes manager Bob Metzler always knew how to entertain his crowds. Attending one of his drag-race, monster-truck, jet-car, stunt extravaganzas, I clicked this human-torch photo. I was told this "stuntman" arrived with a Vega in tow. He made a deal with Metzler and the next thing I know he was sitting in a gas-soaked suit in a broken-down junk Vega. The door was closed and his assistant lit the fire. The Vega was an instant inferno and about 10 seconds later he came out ablaze from the burning Vega. He threw himself on the ground and his assistant put him out. He got to his feet and the crowd cheered!

Tulsa, Oklahoma, 1972
Yes, it's the battle of the dually tow trucks. Jim Paoli (near) versus Don "Stardust" Schumacher. Nobody was hurt. It's a bad day at the races when tow trucks are more exciting than the fuel funny cars on the racetrack.

Inset: OCIR, California, 1972
One of the few rear engine fuel funny cars ever built was owned and driven by Californian Dave Bowman. Dave's *California Stud* Vega Panel was fun to watch, a very exciting ride. Before Dave built the *Stud*, he had an AA/FA named *Mental Cruelty*. It was also fun to watch.

Right: Santa Pod, England, 1978
Slammin' Sammy Miller and his *Vanishinig Point* rocket powered Vega funny car. Sammy was crankin' 300 mph runs back in 1978!

Below: Lakeland, Florida, 1972
Harry Hudson and his *Super Ford* Mustang fuel funny car set their sights on the Christmas tree. Believe it or not, he missed it.

Pomona, California, 1970
Dave Hough starts to litter the race-track with his blower belt. But Dave's *Nanook* AA/FA will clean up after itself – with the parachute.

Irwindale, California, 1970
What goes up must come down. The *King Rat* with Gervis O'Neill at the wheel shows the Irwindale crowd what happens when you come down hard from a wheelstand. He only smacked the guardrail, but walked away pissed.

OCIR, California, 1969

It's either Rusty Delling or Marv Eldridge goin' sideways with the *Fiberglass Trends* fuel funny Javelin. The Javelin looked cool with its candy red paint and gold lettering, but this car was a handful for anyone behind the wheel.

Pomona, California, late 1970s
Clint Miller lights up the *Mountain Monza* fuel funny car. The *Monza* had quite an engine failure. Miller was burned and took a while to heal. He retired from driving soon after.

Riverside, California, 1967
Jim Dunn at speed from the bridge over the track at Riverside. That large spot to the left of Dunn's Top Fueler is his blower pulley. Behind the car is the pulley bracket. I think the pulley ended up in the next county. Nobody was hurt.

Dallas International Raceway, early 1970s
The tree goes green and Dick Shroyer's A/G Anglia Panel becomes a tricycle.

Ontario, Canada, mid-1970s
R. Gaines Markley was very happy he was driving a rear-engined Top Fueler. His big fire only toasted his parachute. Yes, he got stopped and needed more oil in his fuel-burning Hemi.

Indy Nationals, 1969
Rico Paris puts on a show with his Top Gas dragster. Paris bent his racer while "dancing" on the Indy asphalt.

Lodi, California, 1967
Jim Herbert walks away from the *Lizard* Top Fuel dragster. Jim's hands were burned black from the oil fire he just experienced. He soon recovered from his burns and returned to racing.

Pomona, California, early 1990s
Sherm Gunn makes life exciting for photographers. Sherm scraped some paint and stopped a few hearts.

Green Valley Raceway, Texas, 1972
Danny Rightsell finds out how short Green Valley Raceway can be if your chute doesn't open. Into the surplus Navy aircraft carrier net he goes. Danny wasn't hurt, but his racer was bent.

Above: Fremont, California, 1967

If you got *Pure Hell* in the AA/FA class, then you must have *Pure Heaven*. Leon Fitzgerald owned and drove this blown Chevy-powered racer. Match racing with *Pure Hell* was a fan favorite – good versus evil.

Inset: OCIR, California, 1972

"Hand Grenade" Harry Higler lives up to his nickname. Driving the *Sandman* Top Fueler, Harry has a major "boom." Can you find the pieces and parts? Clutch can, injectors, clutch plate, etc. Nobody got hurt!

Left: Fremont, California, 1966-67

Rich Guasco's *Pure Hell* is one bad-ass racecar. This car started one of the wildest classes in drag racing, the AA/FA class. Blown fuel-burning engines in a 98-inch wheelbased racecar. Dale "The Snail" Emory was at the controls.

Bakersfield, California, 1971

Jimmy Inge has major problems with his *Sons of the Rising Sun* Jr. Fueler. Big boom and Jimmy's Jr. Fueler tries to get rid if its engine. He got it stopped and the engine was blown forward on the chassis.

Tulsa, Oklahoma, 1972
Don Garlits hovers in the shutdown area. Yes, all four wheels are in the air.

Fremont, California, 1966
Running over your own fuel tank is not a good thing to do. Noel Black's crew forgot to tie down the fuel tank. Better to run over it on the pushdown than on the run.

Pomona, California, 1968
Paul Pittman's brakes lock on his 1941 BB/GS Willys. Paul had his hands full, but he got the Willys stopped safely.

Fremont, California, 1967
Tommy Fults is a bit out of shape with his Top Fuel dragster. Tommy also drove Unlimited Hydroplanes. Unfortunately, Tommy lost his life in a Hydro.

Indy, 1987

Okay, I know I shot this in the 1980s, but I like the photos. The car was from Oklahoma and the owner's name was Henry. That's all the info I have on the car. This was one of the longest and worst funny car fires I have ever seen. The car lit up before the finish line and burned to the end of the track. Yes, Henry the driver got burned, and yes, it was his retirement run in a fuel funny car.

Indy, mid-1980s

Okay, another 1980s funny car happening. Ron Dudley in the Oklahoma-based *St. Moritz* fuel funny car. Then, BOOM! The fuel tank explodes and all hell breaks loose. The body blows off, that was good for Ron, as it took lots of fire off the driver. Ron was singed, but he walked away.

Martin, Michigan, mid-1970s
The "Golden Greek" Chris Karamesines lights up the Michigan night. The legend of Top Fuel racing has always been a showman. Okay, that's crewman "Pork Chop" trying to ruin my photo.

Gainesville, Florida, 1972
Yes, that's the third member flying out from the rear of Lew Arrington's *Brutus* fuel funny Mustang. Now that is making a lot of horsepower!

Fremont, California, 1966-67
The Warlock heads for the NorCal skies. Herb Pickney is at the controls of Fred Sorensen's awesome AA/FA. He came down hard destroying the oil pan and front end.

Gainesville, Florida, 1972
The end, yes, the end of Mickey Thompson's fuel funny Grand Am. Driver Butch Maas endured the inferno to the end of the track. Butch couldn't get out because his fire boot was caught on the throttle. With the body starting to melt down on him, Butch finally got it loose and dove out of the burning mess.